Ten Little Fish

by AUDREY WOOD

illustrated by BRUCE WOOD

Scholastic Children's Books
Euston House, 24 Eversholt Street
London NW1 1DB
a division of Scholastic Ltd
London ~ New York ~ Toronto ~ Sydney ~ Auckland
Mexico City ~ New Delhi ~ Hong Kong

First published in hardback in the USA by the Blue Sky Press, an imprint of Scholastic Inc., 2004
First published in paperback in the UK by Scholastic Ltd, 2006

Copyright © Audrey Wood and Bruce Wood, 1998

10 digit ISBN 0 439 95110 0

13 digit ISBN 978 0439 95110 4

All rights reserved

Printed at Leo Paper Products, China

2 4 6 8 10 9 7 5 3 1

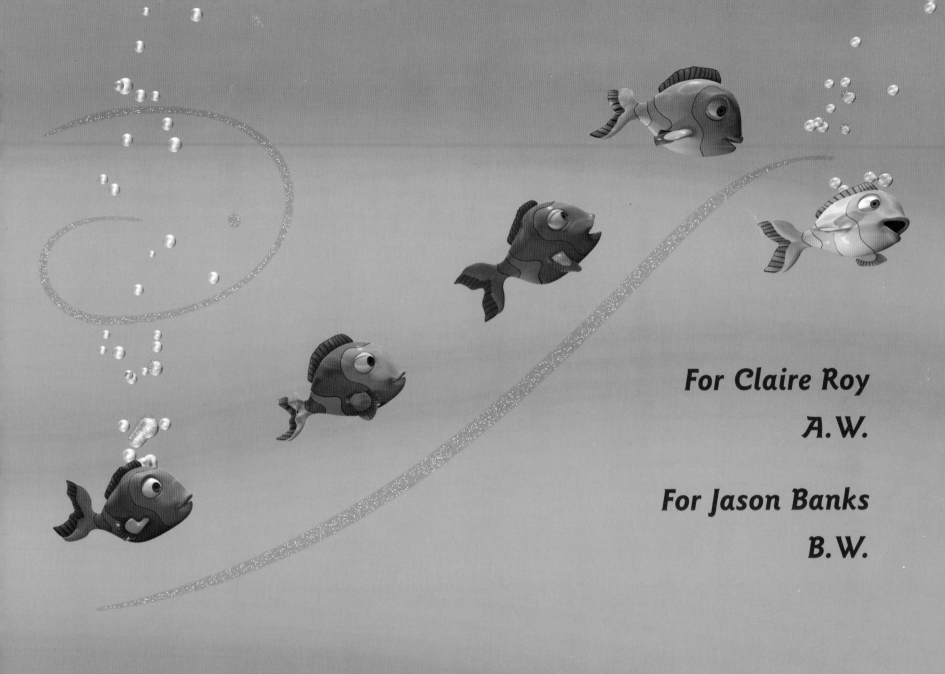

For Claire Roy
A.W.

For Jason Banks
B.W.

Ten Little Fish, swimming in a line.

One dives down, and now there are . . .

Nine Little Fish, swimming past a crate.

One goes in, and now there are . . .

Eight Little Fish, swimming toward heaven.
One jumps up, and now there are . . .

Seven Little Fish, swimming through sticks.

One gets lost, and now there are . . .

Six Little Fish, swimming to survive.
One wants to hide, and now there are . . .

Five Little Fish, swimming by the shore.
One grabs a snack, and now there are . . .

Four Little Fish, swimming out to sea.
One makes a friend, and now there are . . .

Three Little Fish, swimming in the blue.

One waves goodbye, and now there are . . .

Two Little Fish, swimming in the sun.
One takes a nap, and now there's only . . .

One Little Fish.

What will he do?

Along comes another fish, and that makes . . .

Two Little Fish, in love with each other.

Soon one is a father, and the other is a . . .

Mother!
But Mother and Father don't count this time . . .

Just Ten Little Fish – swimming in a line!